Self-Love Letters

Erika Shauna Pereira

BookLeaf Publishing

India | USA | UK

Made with ❤ on the BookLeaf Publishing Platform
www.bookleafpub.in
www.bookleafpub.com

Dedication

Here's to all the people, places and life experiences that inspired me with memories to write about. To my family (mom, dad and Aaron) for always being my biggest supporters, introducing me to the artistic world, and showering me with unconditional love and support. To Zyra, my cute lil' fur-buddy who brings joy to every day like a ray of sunshine.

Remembering my late family members: Grandpa Michael, Aunt Linda, and Fr. Nascimento - who inspired me with their music or writings.

Lastly, here's to **you** and me for spoiling ourselves rotten with self-love like we should!

Preface

Without a doubt, my life's journey has always been full
of plot-twists, wrong turns and surprises. But, love and
kindness have always been my saving grace.
Every poem is inspired by personal moments where I
discovered the importance of love, especially the love I
have for myself.
Every 'love letter' is an ode to all the versions of myself
and elements that I love deeply. The ultimate goal of this
book is to give any one who reads it a reason to smile
and be proud about loving yourself!

Acknowledgements

Shoutout to my soulmate, Paramjit, for constantly encouraging me with everything I do. Your support is the reason why I built the courage to register for the poetry challenge that leads to publishing my first book!

Props to Zyra, for running around our home and keeping me company while I write these poems.

A special thank you to **Noor Rishi**, for the time and effort put into designing the perfect cover art for this book!

Photograph of the author was captured by my wonderful and talented sibling, Aaron Steve Pereira a.k.a **ASP Visuals**.

1. Sunshine

I wake up in the morning,
To sun beams through my window.
The trees sway to the breeze,
And the songbirds say "hello."

What a lovely start to my day!
I set all the right intentions.
Singing along to my favourite songs,
While making breakfast in my kitchen.

Now I'm ready to step outside,
And get a warm hug from sunshine.
Smile at strangers as I make my way
To chase goals, one day at a time.

I see the brighter days ahead,
Now that I made it through all storms.
Yesterday has ended at dusk,
Today is where I belong!

-E.S.P

2. Paper Rocket

It's never too late
to love the life you create,
And take off like a paper rocket.

Stay unstoppable and proud,
Leave your mark on the crowd
As you take the stage and rock it!

Be the go-getter
Who's not afraid of bad weather.
Trust yourself as you take flight.

Don't let adversities hold you down.
Aim for your dreams as you move around,
Soar to newer heights!

-E.S.P

3. School Uniform

Here's to my younger self wearing a school uniform,
Who always had a love for arts and sports.
The naughtiest kid in all classrooms,
Never worried about exam reports.

Remember how we were a "daredevil"?
Who shared meals and laughs at break sessions.
From games, pranks and cheap thrills,
To learning from books and life-long lessons.

I will always admire you for being unfiltered and free,
And love the way you easily made friends.
I still hold all those memories close to me,
Even though nothing stayed the same since then.

Sporting your best smile at our school's farewell,
Saying goodbye to the times that were easier.
Little did you know, bigger lessons start after that final
bell,
And exposure to the real world became your new
teacher.

There's a dream you visioned beyond school gates,
And I live each day to chase it.

Many more challenges came our way,
But you taught me how to face it.

Forgive yourself for all those minor mistakes,
They shaped us into the adult we're meant to be.
I promise you I'll do everything it takes
To always make you proud of me.

-E.S.P

4. LOVE

I realised how wonderful love is
Because it's not just made for two.
Love crosses over all borders,
And resides deep within you!

Love is more than romantic equations,
And goes beyond our stomach butterflies.
There's a whole lot of love in those who stand by you
And hold your hand when everything's awry.

Love comes with indulging in self-care
Like going out on solo walks,
Or a date for one at a cafe,
And pushing yourself with pep-talks!

True love is never dangerous,
Little gestures can be life changing.
Like warm hugs shared with loved ones
or kindness that comes from strangers.

Love is life's sweetest luxury
Well-earned for you and me.
Don't let their rules divide you,

Love is equal and free!

-E.S.P

5. Typewriter

I grew up in a house of poetry,
With a typewriter everyone loved to use.
A young girl once gave into her curiosity,
And decided to write her own muse.

After reading the art works from her loved ones,
She learnt how to write a verse or two.
"Look at my first writing, mom!
It's dedicated to you."

Two lines of love was all it took
For a mother to see a future poet in her little girl.
"Don't ever stop writing, my child.
Someday your words will inspire the world!"

A young dreamer started to pave the way
With every single word that follows.
That little kid who poured her heart out every day,
Knew she's destined to be a writer tomorrow.

-E.S.P

6. Inner Visions

It's a little past midnight,
I'm skinny dipping in my inner visions.
The odds give me a fight,
But I took a shot with my decision

Of escaping the corporate race
And walking on my own path.
Devoted to the mission I chase,
Of shaping my story into art.

With dreams to conquer,
Fears to overcome,
Intrusive thoughts to silence,
I learn and become -

Nothing but the best version of me.
It's alright if I don't fit in.
As long as I turn into the human I desire to be
And awaken my inner vision.

-E.S.P

7. Rainbow

The rain clouds have finally passed by,
And you made it out of the dark.
Here's to appreciating the brighter side,
Smiling under the rainbow arc!

Keep holding on to your inner beauty,
Even when the seasons change.
Be proud of the vibrant masterpiece
Only your personality could paint.

While naysayers could never overshadow
Your parade of love and high hopes.
Dreamers revel in the true colours
Spiraling in your kaleidoscope.

-E.S.P

8. 8

...5,6,7,8!
Swing with the rhythm of every second.
As time slips away through the clock's hands,
The woes turn into passing moments.

Enjoy every step of your transformation.
You were not born to be a lost cause.
The little efforts build your foundation,
Even if you don't get a round of applause.

Every mistake unveils a realisation
That makes you improve your groove.
Dance through the revelations
Leading to your best moves.

With one lifetime and a million dreams,
Turn every fall into a plié for aiming higher.
Don't skip a beat in your own routine
Rewarding you with the future you desire.

-E.S.P

9. Butterfly Effect

It took downfalls to get to my biggest wins,
With life-lessons that always reflect
On how the redirections that came with a whirlwind,
Led to my own butterfly effect.

To my teenage-self who doused her flames,
I will always, always adore you.
You won over every mind-game,
And learned to place no one before you.

After every loss, you rose above,
Shedding old habits and ways.
Thank you for turning grief into love,
Be proud of floating by with grace.

You grew wiser with every passing moon,
Bounced back after every good cry.
Because you protected us like a cocoon,
I evolved into a butterfly.

-E.S.P

10. Skin

My skin writes a pretty poetry
With the beauty marks on my face,
From spots and pores across my body,
To stretch marks leaving their own trace.

Every tan paints a memory
Of summers in paradise.
Every bruise leaves a history,
That inspires me to rise.

Once you read between the fine lines,
And seek the beauty that lies within.
You'll meet the soul that ages gracefully,
while they proudly wear my bare skin.

-E.S.P

11. Festival

I booked a solo ticket to a festival,
Where music lovers united on a Sunday.
Stood in the crowd looking up to my idols,
Hoping to headline like them someday!

All the worries fade as I look at the stage,
Watching artists perform live for you and me.
Our differences are left beyond the gates,
And every passing minute is filled with peace.

We're singing in unison while the clashes outside
Are constantly trying to tear us apart.
Bringing light to hopeful messages that hide
Beyond all the contributions of art.

With smiling faces all around,
I realise what a great time it is to be alive!
All of the love and warmth shared on these grounds,
Will be a souvenir I'll cherish for life.

-E.S.P

12. Warm Fuzzies

I hide from reality in my reading nook,
And dive into the haven of my books.
Sing along to timeless retro bops,
Swing to the melodies playing at gift shops.
Light candles with a fresh scent of wild berries,
Spoil my sweet tooth with cakes kissed by cherries.
Buy myself soft toys and chocolate bouquets,
Weave love into every craft I crochet.
Smile to the thoughts scribbled in handwritten letters,
Or postcards with well-wishes to make me feel better.
Soak up the summer in sundresses,
Seek the cute cats hiding in the hedges.
Got my favourite dates engraved on my rings,
And I revisit memories worth celebrating.
The noise in my head fades as I start to love me,
And relish little joys that give me warm fuzzies.

-E.S.P

13. Stars

Let's always support and love each other,
Just like stars that twinkle together
In a cluster with space for all to shine.

Stay grounded by self-gravity
In a stardust of solidarity.
Trust that the universe will align.

Don't let ambitions fade into the dark,
Achieve everything with your inner spark.
Keep on moving until you breakthrough.

Stay consistent and best believe
Nothing is ever too hard to achieve
If you focus on your point of view.

Failures don't define who we are,
Falls turn you into a shooting star.
Make a wish and turn it into your reality.

Thrive to the fullest under the sky,
Always keep your hopes high.
Let your sparkle brighten up our galaxy.

-E.S.P

14. 4-Leaf Clover

Just like a 4-leaf clover,
I'm as lucky as can be.
Not a soul holds power to walk over
the path I lay out for me.

While pessimists focus on emptiness,
I'm optimistic with my glass half-full.
There's always room for improvement,
While I'm doing the best I could.

I embrace my fate with the fourth leaf
That makes my clover stand out from the rest.
Filled with self-love and the belief
That no goal is too hard to manifest.

-E.S.P

15. Jazz Bar

Oh, how I live for these happy hours!
I put my smile on and wear a silk dress,
Walk right into my go-to jazz bar,
Where the music and energy is always the best.

I get all the fuzzy feelings,
Meeting strangers with a music taste like mine.
Dancing under one ceiling,
While the band sets a mood so divine.

"I'd like to have your best sober drink"
I say as my bar-buddies start wondering
How I have a good time without the vices,
And cherish an evening worth remembering.

The piano man's solo inspires me
To bask in every moment of my life.
Even if it's a mix of black and white keys,
I'll find my own rhythm and improvise.

-E.S.P

16. Onyx

Oh, little onyx, breaking free from the caves.
You carved a story of resilience.
Though the pressure mounted, you stood brave
And moved past hardships with brilliance.

While the crowd drowned in mediocrity,
You mystified them with your charm.
Never settled for a fate that's ordinary,
Always protected yourself from harm.

You own your chaotic patterns with pride,
And turn darkness into your magical realm.
A passerby may see the rock outside,
But lovers discover the hidden gem.

-E.S.P

17. Empty Beach

After ditching all the parties and crowd,
I found solace at an empty beach.
Knowing that I am safe and sound,
Even if my phone is out of reach.

Chasing golden hours on a weekday.
I took a solo ride with my blue scooty
Visited a quaint bar by the bay,
Sipped on mocktails so fruity.

Now I'm building sandcastles like a happy child,
While the waves splash on my wavy hair.
Catching little memories that make me smile
So much that my problems disappear.

I listened to the ocean's symphonies,
And watched birds fly to their nest.
Soaked in the beauty of simplicity
As the day ends at sunset.

-E.S.P

18. Disco Ball

I love disco balls with broken pieces
That stand alone and still shine.
They inspired me to make peace with
The scattered thoughts in my mind.

The past maybe filled with sorrows,
But I have a million reasons to smile.
So I start embracing my own glow,
And chase thrills that make it all worthwhile.

I keep dazzling through the still nights,
No one can tame my inner flare.
Throw me under a global spotlight,
I'll leave a sparkle everywhere.

With my feet rooted in the present,
I let love keep spinning around.
Making a statement with my presence,
Leaving every stranger spellbound.

Creating happy endings after tough days,
Spreading a joy that's everlasting.
No matter what music life plays,

Best believe, I'll keep on dancing.

-E.S.P

19. Flower Power

I am as strong as a little flower
With delicate and bright petals.
My fragility holds power,
And my love never settles.

I outgrow the thorns as I bloom,
And enjoy the warmth of the sun.
Dance to the rains in June,
And leave my mark on everyone.

Through the new beginnings,
I blossom unapologetically.
Despite the flower pickers and bee stings,
I radiate vibrant energies.

-E.S.P

20. Miles Away

I remember moving out of my city like it was yesterday,
No full-proof plan for the next destination.
Took a taxi on a journey that's miles away,
With a heart full of faith and anticipation.

I turned away from roadblocks,
And let the bad bridges burn.
Navigated out of dead-ends,
Found the right track with every U-turn.

I still have many miles to go,
And I make every move with intent.
Trusting that the universe guides me
Towards a route that makes me content.

4 years ago, I turned my story around.
Settled in the place I call my **second home**.
Despite wandering through the ups and downs,
I can proudly say I made it on my own!

-E.S.P

21. Paradise

Inspiration always unravels
From the landscapes in front of me.
When I took the roads less traveled,
It led to my best discoveries.

While they're afraid to test waters,
I don't think it is that deep.
I've always been a go-getter,
Labeled as the black sheep.

I took risks and explored the unknown,
Trusting that the universe has my back.
Fell, but learned how to rise on my own,
Like a wildflower blooming through the cracks.

Now I'm floating with my dream clouds,
Everyday under the endless skies.
Making my older versions proud,
As I live in my own paradise.

I tossed a message in a bottle into the ocean,
To guide you out of the blue.
If you're ever drowning in waves of emotions,

I hope my letters save **you**!

25

-E.S.P

22. HOME: (A Bonus Letter!)

Welcome to adulthood!
The chapter you once anticipated.
It's time to close bad doors for good,
And honour the lifestyle you created.

Build a home and decorate the rooms
With elements you treasure.
Turn up your music that sets the mood,
Appreciate simple pleasures.

After all the parties came to an end,
You finally found peace in your zone.
Solitude became your new best friend,
Who says you can't be happy alone?

You've set all the right boundaries,
Kept your space and energies clean.
From self-care to doing your laundry,
You've mastered your daily routine.

Though reality strikes without guidelines,
You're the captain of every right direction.
Cheers to independence and good times,

In a house full of love and affection!

27

-E.S.P